P9-DLZ-213

TOWNSHIP OF UNION
FREE PUBLIC LIBRARY

SECRETS
FROM
THE
ROCKS

SECRETS FROM THE ROCKS

TOWNSHIP OF UNION
FREE PUBLIC LIBRARY

DINOSAUR HUNTING
with
Roy Chapman Andrews

by

Albert Marrin

DUTTON CHILDREN'S BOOKS / New York

Copyright © 2002 by Albert Marrin

All rights reserved. No part of this publication may be reproduced or transmitted
in any form or by any means, electronic or mechanical, including photocopy, recording,
or any information storage and retrieval system now known or to be invented, without permission
in writing from the publisher, except by a reviewer who wishes to quote brief passages in
connection with a review written for inclusion in a magazine, newspaper, or broadcast.

Library of Congress Cataloging-in-Publication Data

Marrin, Albert

Secrets from the rocks: dinosaur hunting with Roy Chapman Andrews / Albert Marrin.—1st ed.

p.   cm.

Includes bibliographical references.

Summary: A biography of the scientist-adventurer, Roy Chapman Andrews,

focusing on the expeditions he led for New York's American Museum of Natural History

to the Gobi Desert in Mongolia in an effort to uncover dinosaur fossils.

ISBN 0-525-46743-2

1. Andrews, Roy Chapman, 1884–1960—Juvenile literature.

2. Paleontologists—United States—Biography—Juvenile literature. 3. Dinosaurs—Juvenile literature.
[1. Andrews, Roy Chapman, 1884–1960. 2. Naturalists. 3. Paleontologists. 4. Dinosaurs.] I. Title.

QE707.A53 M37 2002   560'.92—dc21   [B]   2001047084

Published in the United States by Dutton Children's Books,

a division of Penguin Putnam Books for Young Readers

345 Hudson Street, New York, New York 10014

www.penguinputnam.com

Designed by Heather Wood

Printed in China

First Edition

1   3   5   7   9   10   8   6   4   2

PHOTO CREDITS

Abbreviations used: **American Museum of Natural History {AMNH};**

James B. Shackelford {JBS}; Roy Chapman Andrews {RCA}.

Front cover: JBS, AMNH #411005; Endpapers: JBS,
AMNH #410771; Half title: JBS, AMNH #410927; Frontispiece: JBS, AMNH #410722;
Dedication page: JBS, AMNH #258329; Opposite Contents page: JBS, AMNH #410933;
Opposite p.1: Walter Granger, AMNH #108726; p. 3 Courtesy of Beloit Historical Society;
p. 6 RCA, AMNH #218409; p. 7 RCA, AMNH #219165; p. 9 J. Otis Wheelock, AMNH #31598;
p. 14 RCA, AMNH #228955; p. 15 Yvette Borup Andrews, AMNH #241736; p. 16 JBS, AMNH
#410703; p. 17 Yvette Borup Andrews, AMNH #242014; p. 18 RCA, AMNH #251455; p. 23 JBS,
AMNH #411031; p. 24 JBS, AMNH #411042; p. 28 RCA, AMNH #251465; p. 29 AMNH
#284790; p. 31 JBS, AMNH #410699; p. 32 Yvette Borup Andrews, AMNH #241904; p. 35 RCA,
AMNH #251593; p. 38 JBS, AMNH #410767; p. 39 RCA, AMNH #251629; p. 41 JBS, AMNH #410765;
p. 42 JBS, AMNH #410763; p. 45 JBS, AMNH #410737; p. 47 JBS, AMNH #258384; p. 49 JBS,
AMNH #411005; p. 54 JBS, AMNH #410902; p. 57 Julius Kirschner, AMNH #314510

ENDPAPERS: *Land of the big sky.*
The Central Asiatic Expeditions camped in the Gobi Desert.

HALF TITLE: *Portrait of an explorer.*
*The Gobi Desert was not only a very rugged place but a
dangerous one, infested with bandits and renegade Chinese soldiers.
Roy Chapman Andrews and his men carried guns for protection.*

FRONTISPIECE: *On the move. Expedition vehicles
making their way across a low ridge on the Gobi Desert.*

DEDICATION PAGE: *Merin, leader of the camel caravan
for the Central Asiatic Expeditions, looking at pictures of
the expeditions that appeared in a magazine.*

OPPOSITE CONTENTS PAGE: *Expedition members often had
animal pets to ease their loneliness. Besides a large black vulture
named Connie, Roy Chapman Andrews adopted some eagle chicks.
Here he is feeding them chunks of meat with chopsticks.*

FOR THE AMERICAN MUSEUM OF NATURAL HISTORY,
IN GRATITUDE FOR THE WONDERFUL WORK IT HAS DONE FOR CHILDREN
FOR OVER A CENTURY

Contents

The Making of an Explorer

The world we see today is not the world as it has always been. In prehistoric times the Earth was a very different place.

If we could board a time machine and travel, say, 225 million years into the past, we would hardly recognize Earth. Great mountain ranges, such as the Rockies, Andes, and Himalayas, had not yet formed. Continents were closer together than they are today. Salty, shallow seas reached far inland, bordered by endless swamps and jungles. There were no flowers or grasses or trees whose leaves changed color and fell off when the weather turned cool. Only giant ferns and trees that looked like modern-day palms covered the land. Ice had not formed at the North and South Poles. Nearly everywhere the climate was warm and humid the year round. There were no people anywhere.

Fantastic creatures roamed our planet back then. This was a world of dinosaurs (meaning "terrible lizards") and pterosaurs ("winged lizards"), flying reptiles with wingspans ten feet across, bulging eyes, and sawlike teeth. Fifty-foot-long reptiles called plesiosaurs ("near lizards"), powered by immense paddlelike limbs, prowled the sea in search of prey. Placodonts ("flat teeth"), turtlelike animals with shells wide enough on which to park a modern-day truck, hunted fish far out at sea. Dragonflies with bodies a foot long and wings two feet across darted through the air.

How do we know about this lost world? What proof do we have that these creatures ever really existed? How did they develop over time? How did they live? Why did they vanish?

People who try to answer such questions are a special breed. Part scientist and part adventurer, they go to the far corners of the world, hunting for the remains of prehistoric life.

Roy Chapman Andrews was one of them. A man who lived life to the fullest, he had boundless energy and faith in himself. The expeditions he led unearthed the remains

Expedition vehicles and tents in the Gobi badlands. In front are eroded—worn away—sides of a gully, a prime site for fossil hunting.

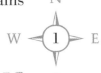

of animals unlike any ever seen by human eyes. He also introduced Americans and Europeans to the people of Central Asia.

Roy never said much about his boyhood years; he did not think it important. As a rule, he believed that nothing of much interest happens until a person goes into the world on his own. When asked about his life, he would chuckle. He suffered, he said, from a rare disease— "exploritis." That is not a true sickness; Roy invented it to describe himself. "I was born to be an explorer," he explained. "There never was any decision to make. I couldn't do anything else and be happy."

Born in Beloit, Wisconsin, on January 26, 1884, Roy began exploring early. He tells us in *Under a Lucky Star*, his autobiography, that his favorite book was Daniel Defoe's *Robinson Crusoe*, a novel about a castaway on a desert island. Roy's mother read it to him more than a dozen times, and he remembered every detail of it for the rest of his life. He used to think that nothing would be so marvelous as living on a secluded island with wild animals, shifting for himself.

Even as a toddler, Roy could not stay put for long. "I was like a rabbit," he recalled, "happy only when I could run out-of-doors. To stay in the house was torture to me

then, and it has been ever since. Whatever the weather, in sun or rain, calm or storm, day or night, I was outside, unless my parents almost literally locked me in." Roy said that he "loved nature so passionately" that he could not stay out of the woods near his home. As he grew, he wandered there alone, turning over rocks to see what lived under them. He carried field glasses and a notebook to describe the birds and animals he saw.

Roy also had a single-barrel shotgun, which his father gave him on his ninth birthday and taught him how to use safely. The youngster saw it as a tool for collecting specimens—samples—of animals for future study. Today, we have other ways of learning about wild creatures than shooting them. With high-speed cameras and telescopic lenses, we can record their behavior from a safe distance. Catching an animal and releasing it with a small radio attached to its body allows scientists to track its movements and learn about its habits. Nevertheless, the only way to study an animal's internal body structure is to dissect a specimen.

Roy mounted birds and small animals he collected, following the instructions in a book on taxidermy, the art of preparing skins so they appear lifelike. Taxidermy allowed him to learn about each creature in a "hands-on" way. He saw how its muscles, bones, blood vessels, nerves, and vital organs—heart, brain, liver, lungs—related to one another.

He added to his weekly allowance of ten cents by mounting birds and deer heads for hunters during the shooting season. Hunters did not shoot animals to study them but to get trophies to impress their friends and display in their homes. A century ago, "fashionable" people decorated their homes in this way. Bearskin rugs, heads and all, covered floors. Elephant feet served as umbrella stands. Deer heads with long antlers hung on walls. President Theodore Roosevelt, an avid hunter, displayed scores of animal heads on the walls of his house.

As the years passed, the boy grew into a handsome young man. Over six feet tall, Roy was lean and athletic, with blue eyes and brown hair. A calm person, he had a relaxed manner and a good sense of humor. He smiled easily. People liked him.

When Roy turned eighteen, he enrolled in Beloit College, near his home. College was not the greatest success of his life. Roy joined a student fraternity, partied a lot, and went in for sports in a big way. His favorite subjects were literature and the sciences: biology, geology, geography, chemistry. These came easily, and he enjoyed

At twenty, Roy was a student at Beloit College, Wisconsin. He made friends easily, enjoyed sports, was popular with girls, and studied just enough to pass his subjects.

them. "Most of the other subjects bored me exceedingly, and I worked just hard enough to get minimum grades," he admitted. Yet he never lost sight of his goal of becoming an explorer.

Two months after graduating in 1906, Roy took a train to New York City. More than anything, he wanted to work for the American Museum of Natural History. The museum, which opened its doors in 1877, has always had a double mission. First, its scientists collect specimens, study them, and add to our knowledge of the natural world and humanity's place in it. Equally important, the museum's exhibits educate the public about the natural world in the most interesting ways possible. Each year, crowds of people pass through its exhibition halls, marveling at the displays. Most visitors never know that these are only a tiny part of its holdings. Like all great museums, most of its work goes on in offices and laboratories that visitors never see.

For every specimen on display, the museum keeps many more in collections reserved for study by experts in their fields. Today, it has over 34 million specimens representing every aspect of life on Earth. It has more birds, bugs, and spiders than any other museum. It keeps countless snakes and frogs in jars of formaldehyde, a liquid preservative. You can see a herd of seven African elephants, mounted in lifelike poses, and a family group of lions. There is a collection of shrunken human heads the size of your fist and a group of thirty-five human heads tattooed with zigzag designs. Then there are the dinosaur

bones—the largest collection anywhere. Many of these were found by expeditions led by Roy Chapman Andrews.

Arriving in New York with thirty-five dollars in his pocket, Roy hurried to the museum. Shortly before graduation, he had written the director, Dr. Hermon C. Bumpus, asking about job openings. Told that there were none, even for college graduates, Roy decided to show up anyhow. When Dr. Bumpus said there were still no openings, Roy recalled that "my heart dropped into my shoes." But only for a moment. Thinking quickly, he offered to wash the floors. Those floors were not just any floors. They were museum floors. "I'll clean them and love it if you'll let me," he said. He spoke as if he meant it. And he did!

That little speech got him a job, at forty dollars a month, in the Department of Taxidermy. Every morning, Roy scrubbed floors until they shone. From noon to closing time, he prepared specimens and helped set up exhibits. On some weekday nights he took the subway uptown to Columbia University. There he took extra courses in his main field of interest, zoology—the branch of biology that deals with animal structure, habits, and development.

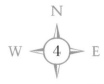

From Whales to Fossils

oy's big break came sooner than he expected. Whales were the reason. Nowadays, we do not kill whales to study them. Nor did scientists do so back then; it was too hard and costly to send an expedition to sea for that purpose. Occasionally, the bodies of whales that had died of natural causes washed ashore, and scientists studied them. That is what happened in 1907, when the museum sent Roy and a helper to bring back a whale found dead on a Long Island beach. Their orders: "Get the whole thing . . . every bone!" After fishermen stripped off the meat and blubber, the two men dismantled the skeleton and put it on a train bound for New York City.

Whales fascinated Roy, who read everything he could find about them in the museum library. He soon realized how little science knew about these marvelous creatures. Zoologists had hardly studied them in the wild; they did not even know how many types, or species, of whale there were.

Luckily for Roy, the museum wanted to expand its holdings of whale skeletons. Its zoologists needed skeletons to study how whales grew and to learn how one species differed from another. So, in 1908, the museum sent Roy to collect specimens of Pacific Ocean whales, not as a member of any expedition but by himself. He loved the idea of exploring on his own.

Roy sailed aboard ships based at Alaskan, Canadian, and Japanese seaports. Called "whalers," these ships were part of the commercial whaling industry, hunting the sea giants for their meat, bones, and fat, called "blubber." Whale meat, a delicacy in Asia, brought high prices. The animals' blubber was melted and then burned in oil lamps to give light. Their bones, ground into meal, made excellent fertilizer.

A poor sailor, Roy found whaling rough going even at the best of times. Constantly seasick, he also had several brushes with death. The nearest came on a dock as a crane was lifting a whole whale carcass that a ship had towed into port. The carcass slipped from a tackle, crushing the man standing beside him. "He could hardly be recognized as a human being," Roy recalled. "I was standing near him and only escaped a similar fate by leaping off the dock into twenty feet of water as the carcass crashed upon us."

Yet Roy would not give up. During each voyage, he watched, photographed, and measured whales. He timed

A poor sailor, Roy often got seasick during his voyages aboard whaling ships. This picture was taken in October 1913, when he was twenty-nine years old.

them to see how long they stayed on the surface, how often they dived, and how long they remained underwater. Roy drew diagrams of how they used their flippers and flukes. He described their mating habits, which no scientist had ever done. "I felt embarrassed to be spying on their love-making like a Peeping Tom," he said, but he did it anyhow —for science. Roy tasted the milk of a mother whale that had been killed when a bomb-tipped harpoon exploded inside her; the milk was bitter. Once he crawled into the belly of a dead whale to see how it felt. It was dark and slippery. Every month or so, he sent crates of neatly labeled bones by steamship to New York. Some of the specimens that he collected still hang in the museum's Hall of Ocean Life. Between whale-hunting seasons, he

Roy took this photo of Japanese workers hoisting a gray whale carcass out of the water onto a dock. Later, other workers would cut it up for use as food, lamp oil, and fertilizer.

went off to explore Korea, Burma, southern China, and French Indochina, today's Vietnam.

After returning to the United States in 1913, Roy received a master's degree in zoology from Columbia University. In 1916, he published his first book, *Whale Hunting with Gun and Camera*. This book is chock-full of photographs of whales and whale hunting; it is still a joy to read. By then, he was thirty-two years old and an authority on whales. Yet he was also restless, which led him to make a life-changing decision. He decided that he knew all he needed to know about whales. It was time to try something else. But what?

The museum's president, Dr. Henry Fairfield Osborn, had an idea. Osborn's studies had convinced him that the first humans had lived in Central Asia, and that it was the birthplace of much of the world's animal life on land. From there, Osborn believed, the various life-forms had spread across the planet over land bridges that once linked the continents. Roy felt his chief was right. Yet he also knew that a feeling is not a proof. To be able to say that something in nature is true, you must have evidence, good evidence. Fossils are a key type of evidence about life in the distant past.

About Fossils

Most living things vanish after they die. Bacteria nearly always devour their remains, leaving not a trace. We call this "decay." Yet sometimes, if conditions are right, the remains of a few will be left behind. We call these naturally preserved remains of ancient life-forms "fossils." The word comes from the Latin *fossilis*, for "something dug up."

People have known about fossils for a long time.

The writings of Chinese druggists, dating from around 3000 B.C., contain the earliest known descriptions of fossil bones. Called "dragon bones," they were (and still are) ground up for use in traditional Chinese medicines. Fossils may also help explain the giants and monsters mentioned in the folklore of various peoples. For example, they may have given birth to the legend of the griffins—beasts said to resemble "lions with the beak and wings of

In 1907, Roy (foreground) and a team of taxidermists prepared a life-size model, seventy-six feet long, of a blue whale made of papier-mâché over a framework of angle irons, wood, and wire mesh.

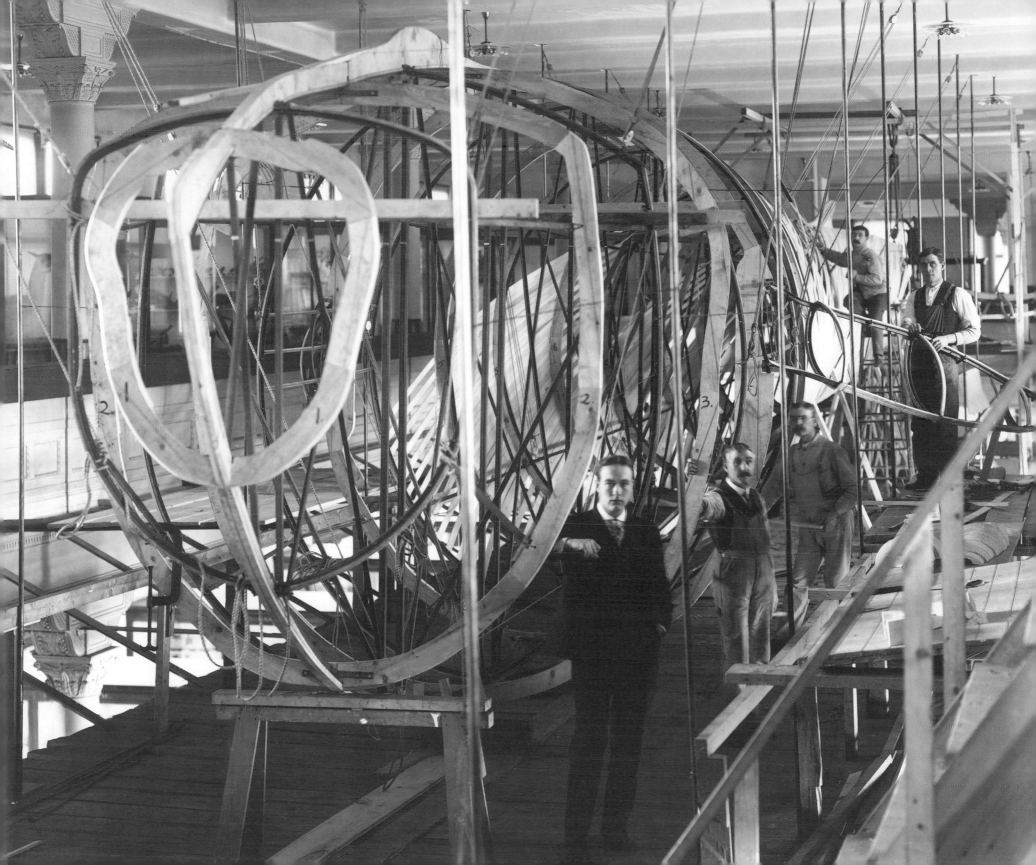

an eagle." Ancient Greeks and Romans displayed fossilized bones in their temples. We do not know what animals these bones came from, nor their age. Yet the ancients recognized them as parts of creatures that did not exist anymore.

We seldom find a complete fossil. Generally, only the hard parts of living things survive. These include bones, teeth, and the shells of animals, and the woody parts of plants. Other fossils are not *parts* of animals or plants at all, but rather animals' or plants' imprints left in mud that hardened before the prints disappeared. Scientists have collected fossils on all continents, including Antarctica. Today, frigid winds blast Antarctica, and sheets of ice thousands of feet thick cover the land. Millions of years ago, however, it had tropical forests and swamps. Fossil fuels like coal, oil, and natural gas formed from the fossilized remains of plants that lived back then. Now they are valuable resources that eventually will run out.

The fossils most prized by scientists, because they tell us so much about the distant past, are the skeletons of prehistoric animals. Let's suppose that an animal died millions of years ago. Usually, other animals—scavengers—would feed on its body, tearing its flesh and crushing its bones. However, once in a while, wind and water might get to the body first, quickly burying it under layers of mud, sand, and gravel. We call these layers "sediments."

Now time passes—a very long time. The constant build-up of sediments on top of one another eventually compresses, or squeezes, the lower layers into sedimentary rock such as sandstone, shale, and limestone. Water seeping through cracks in the rocks slowly dissolves the chemicals in the bones, replacing them with minerals carried in the water. Gradually, the bones lose most of their original material and turn to stone. Occasionally, minerals fossilize bits of skin before the skin can decay. Even dung may be mineralized and turn into a fossil called "coprolite." The largest coprolite ever found is nearly sixteen inches long.

A fossil's color depends on what minerals formed it. Colors range from light gray to red to black. Fossilized tree trunks, like those found in the Petrified Forest of Arizona, have bright rainbow colors arranged in stripes. Yet not all fossils are visible to the naked eye. The oldest fossils are of organisms that lived nearly four billion years ago and are visible only through a microscope.

Scientists called "paleontologists" study fossils for clues to Earth's past environment, climate, and life-forms. An expert can "read" a fossil almost as though it were a page in a book—a mystery book. A fossil can give clues to an animal's size, appearance, and lifestyle. Two long hind legs, for example, suggest a swift runner. Long, daggerlike teeth and claws tapering to sharp points suggest a carnivore, an animal that eats other animals; many carnivore skeletons show signs of combat-related injuries. Broad teeth, good for grinding up vegetation, imply a herbivore, or plant-eater. Finding fossils in a certain layer of rock suggests how long ago the animals lived. Usually, fossils from deeper rock layers are older than those from layers closer to the surface. Yet earthquakes may force the older rock layers to the surface, burying the younger ones beneath them. So position is not always a clue to age. Finding the same type of fossils in different places gives clues to how far the animals may have roamed.

First Trips to the Gobi Desert

If Dr. Osborn was right, there should be fossils in the Gobi Desert of Mongolia, and Roy hoped to find them. The nation of Mongolia—also known as Outer Mongolia—has two neighbors. The Russian territory of Siberia lies to its north. To the south lies a region called Inner Mongolia, ruled by China since the 1600s. Located on a high plateau, or tableland, Mongolia is roughly two thousand miles from east to west and twelve hundred miles from north to south. The Gobi (gobi means "empty space" in Mongolian) covers the country's southern half and extends into Chinese Inner Mongolia. It is three times the size of California.

Until the 1920s, only one fossil had ever been found in the Gobi—a rhinoceros bone from Chinese Inner Mongolia. So at first glance, the Gobi seemed a poor place to search for fossils. But, then again, no expedition had ever gone there to search in a thorough, organized way.

In some ways scientists must also be gamblers. To investigate something, scientists go beyond what is already known. That is what Roy and his boss planned to do. Both men had a hunch, a gut feeling, that they were on the right track. "The fossils are there. I know they are," said Dr. Osborn, patting Roy's shoulder. "Go and find them."

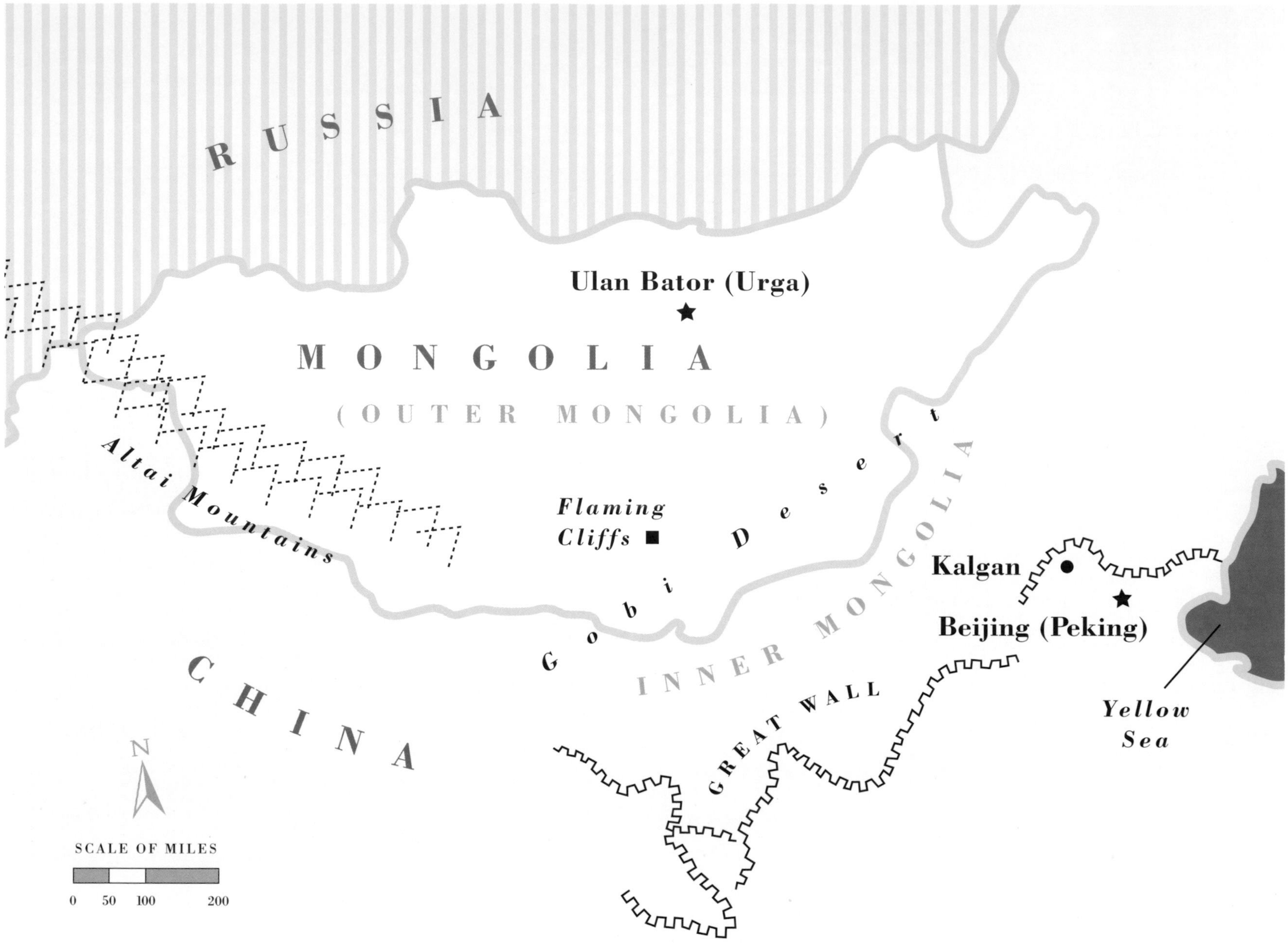

RUSSIA

Ulan Bator (Urga) ★

MONGOLIA

(OUTER MONGOLIA)

Altai Mountains

Flaming
Cliffs ■

Gobi Desert

INNER MONGOLIA

Kalgan ●

Beijing (Peking) ★

Yellow
Sea

CHINA

GREAT WALL

N

SCALE OF MILES

0   50   100   200

N
W — 12 — E
S

SECRETS FROM THE ROCKS

That was easier said than done. The Gobi Desert is a harsh place. Temperatures range from very hot to very cold. In July and August, its low-lying areas heat up like furnaces. In 1883, the Russian explorer Nickolay Przhevalsky recorded a temperature of 113°F in the shade. "In the daytime," he wrote, "the heat enveloped us on all sides, above from the sun, below from the burning ground. On these days the cloudless sky was of a dirty hue, the soil heated to 145° and even higher where the sands are entirely bare." On the other hand, winter lows dip to - 40° F; touching subzero metal will cause flesh to stick to it.

The Gobi is not a sea of loose, shifting sand like the Sahara Desert of Africa. Although the Gobi has large sandy areas, its floor is mostly fine gravel covered by patches of short grass and low thornbushes. Dotted with small lakes, the desert gets up to eight inches of rain a year.

Travel in Mongolia has never been easy. In the early 1900s, it was an ordeal. Mongolia had no paved roads, nor does it have any today in most places. There were only trails used by nomads. The Chinese called these nomads "People of the Wilderness." Nomads had no fixed homes but moved about to graze their sheep herds. They traveled on horse-back; camels carried their belongings. Chinese caravans brought trade goods to the market at Urga (now Ulan Bator, or "Red Hero"), Mongolia's capital.

Over the centuries, few foreigners had visited Mongolia. The Chinese monk Fa-hsien crossed the Gobi in the year A.D. 399 on his way to India. "So far as the eye can reach," he reported, "the route is marked out by the bleached bones of men who have perished in the attempt to cross the desert." Eight centuries later, little had changed. When the Italian traveler Marco Polo crossed the Gobi on his way from Mongolia to China in the 1280s, he found it a "forbidding" place. Even in modern times, few foreigners, mostly Russian explorers and Chinese traders, had traveled across this vast land. Since outsiders knew so little about the Gobi, Roy decided to learn more about it before mounting an expedition.

So in 1917 and 1919, Roy led small parties into Mongolia. On these trips, Roy brought his wife along. The former Yvette Borup, she was the sister of an explorer who had joined Robert E. Peary in the first expedition to reach the North Pole in 1909. An able photographer, Yvette experimented with early types of color film.

The parties followed the caravan trail from Chinese Inner Mongolia to Urga in two automobiles. Hardly any motorcars had ever done that before. As they went, Roy

Roy's first wife, Yvette Borup Andrews, feeding a baby bear on one of their early trips. They later divorced.

shot and trapped hundreds of specimens for museum scientists to study. Antelope, however, were a real challenge. Whenever he drove parallel to a herd of grazing antelope, it exploded in a burst of speed. "They did not run," he recalled. "They simply *flew* across the ground, their legs showing only as a blur. . . . They could not have been traveling less than fifty-five or sixty miles an hour, for they were running in a semicircle about the car while we were moving at forty miles in a straight line."

Yet Roy never hunted as a "sportsman." Sportsmen, he felt, were big show-offs who shot animals to prove their manhood. The explorer knew exactly who he was and did not have to kill to prove anything to himself. "I never have killed except for food and specimens," he wrote. "I have

Getting fresh meat was no problem in the Gobi Desert. A crack shot with a rifle and a skilled horseback rider, Roy usually brought game, like this antelope, back to camp.

shot during my entire life. It has been part of my job. Many thousands of birds and animals have fallen to my gun, but for every one there was a real cause. I find no pleasure in killing just to try my skill."

Mongolia made a deep impression. Roy always remembered those first days there. "Never again will I have such a feeling as Mongolia gave me," he said. Plains shimmering in noonday heat. Glowing orange sunsets. At night the Milky Way a splash of diamonds sparkling on a black-velvet sky. This was paradise—to the explorer. "I had found my country. The one I had been born to know and love."

Mongolians were and are solidly built people with broad faces, high cheekbones, and small eyes. Colorful and rugged, they wore woolen robes dyed yellow, violet, and green. Back then, the only difference between men's and women's outfits was that men wore a belt around the waist, while women allowed their robes to hang loosely about them. On their heads they often sported tall felt hats, studded with Chinese jade and silver, that came to a point at the top. On their feet they wore extra-large boots, which allowed them to add several pairs of woolen socks in cold weather. That made walking difficult. No matter. Whenever they had to go any distance, even a hundred yards, they went on horseback.

The expeditions relied upon hired Mongolians to do basic work, like hauling supplies and setting up camp. They quickly learned how to use Western things. Here a group listens to a phonograph.

Mongolian women took pride in their hair. On special occasions, they braided it and wove it through wooden frames in elaborate headdresses.

Boys and girls learned to ride early. Fathers would tie their four-year-olds to a horse's back for mile-long races at top speed. If the child fell off, up he or she went again, tied a little more tightly than before. Such training, Roy believed, made Mongolians the best horseback riders in the world. He observed that they usually rode at a trot or a full gallop, easily covering fifty miles a day. Roy admired

Roy and his wife, Yvette, once escaped being eaten alive by Mongolian wild dogs similar to this one.

these people of the wilderness. He wrote: "They were a wild, independent folk, hard living, virile, meeting life in the raw. . . . The cowboys of our own early western days were their counterparts."

Each family had three or four shaggy black dogs. By day their masters kept these savage watchdogs chained to stakes driven into the ground. At night, they let them loose to guard the camp from strangers. Similar dogs ran wild in packs.

The wild dogs had a taste for human flesh. Since Mongolians believed evil spirits lived in dead bodies, they did not bury corpses. When a person died, relatives left the corpse on the ground for the dogs to eat. Roy found crushed human bones near old campsites and scattered on the plain outside Urga. Once he timed a dog pack in action; it devoured a corpse in seven minutes. Given the chance, wild dogs would also eat living people.

Wild dogs nearly made a feast of Roy and his wife. As they slept in their sleeping bags beside a campfire, a sound woke Yvette. Talk about luck! When she looked up, she saw fourteen big dogs, their eyes shining in the firelight. They were about to attack the sleepers.

Yvette cried out. Her husband woke with a start and grabbed his rifle. Firing blindly, Roy hit the pack's leader square in the head, killing it instantly. Other shots hit two more dogs, making them limp away into the night. Moments later, horrible howling came from the darkness as the pack ate the injured dogs. Roy dragged the dead leader far from the fire. In the morning, he found only cracked bones and clumps of hair.

Roy did not complain. Danger was simply part of his job. Anyhow, exploring sometimes seemed a lot safer than other activities—like living in a modern city! Roy said New York at night felt more dangerous than camping in the wilds of Mongolia. He spoke from experience. When leaving the museum late one night, he had walked into the middle of a shoot-out between police officers and gangsters on a side street.

Roy's expeditions of 1917 and 1919 made no scientific breakthroughs. Yet they showed Roy the difficulties that a full-scale expedition would face. With that knowledge, he returned to New York. Working day and night, he drew up plans for what he called the Central Asiatic Expeditions—CAE for short. Little did Roy know, then, that the CAE would last a total of eight years, from 1922 to 1930. Of course, it did not stay in the field all that time. At the end of each exploring season, it left the Gobi to rest, refit, and see that its specimens went off safely to the American Museum of Natural History back in New York.

Like most expedition leaders from developed countries in his day, Roy believed he had a right to go wherever he pleased in the name of "science." A patriotic American, he felt that every discovery enhanced his country's image in the world. So, like other leaders, he treated his expeditions' discoveries as sunken treasure—that is, finders keepers. We do not know how local people felt about this attitude; it may have offended them. Nowadays, many countries treat fossil specimens as national treasures, part of their natural heritage.

Launching the Central Asiatic Expeditions

Dr. Osborn had chosen Roy to head the CAE because he was so well qualified. An able zoologist and experienced traveler, he also had a gift for getting people to work together. If people disagreed, somehow he always managed to smooth things over. A man wise enough to know his limitations, he respected experts in their various fields of science. Equally important, he was a genius at raising money. Scientific expeditions cost plenty of money, which the museum did not have. However, Roy asked wealthy people like banker J. P. Morgan and oil tycoon John D. Rockefeller to pick up most of the bills. If they did, he promised, they would go down in history as generous people who advanced the frontiers of human knowledge. Few turned him down.

Roy set out to make exploring history. The CAE would be the largest land expedition ever to leave the United States. Fossil hunting, of course, would be its chief focus. But Roy had even bigger ideas. He wanted to study the natural history of the Mongolian plateau from every angle, past and present. The expedition would map the unexplored parts of the Gobi and collect its living plants and animals. When it finished, he said, science would have a detailed picture of one of the world's least-known regions.

Scientific expeditions don't just happen. In Roy's day, as in our own, preparation is as important as the actual journey. Leaders know they will face many problems. First, Roy had to decide whom to take along. When the press described his plan, applications poured into his office at the museum. In all, ten thousand people asked to join the CAE. Retired soldiers wanted to go for the adventure. A man offered to be Roy's personal butler; he would serve meals in a tuxedo, in the desert, he wrote. Boys begged for a chance to show their courage. *I can climb trees and don't get dizzy*, wrote one. *I know you will meet terrible dangers. Probably wild cannaballs* [cannibals] *will try to eat you. Who knows, I might even save your life.*

The return mail brought most applicants a printed letter of rejection. Roy had nothing against them personally; they seemed decent enough. Yet they were not the sort of people he was looking for.

Roy was inventing a new way of organizing scientific expeditions. Normally, expedition members did several jobs besides their own specialty. For example, a person trained to make maps might also have to row a boat, hunt

SECRETS FROM THE ROCKS

game for food, and shoe the expedition's horses. This made sense because expeditions were usually small. If somebody got sick or died, another person could easily take over. Yet doing more than one job left less time for science. Roy's "team" approach changed all that.

During his two earlier visits to the Gobi, he had realized that the CAE would have to "drop out" of the world for many months at a time. There would be no newspapers, no telephone calls, no mail from home. Radio was in its infancy. Mongolia had no railroads to haul supplies or take out anyone who got sick. Airplanes in those days were too small to carry much cargo; besides, Mongolia had no airfields. When a scientific problem came up, as it must, Roy wanted experts from various fields of science to try to solve it on the spot. Mostly likely they would succeed. If not, they would put it aside for future study in New York.

Roy selected his team carefully. Although, as time went on, the number of expedition members changed from year to year, it was usually about forty men. A majority of them, twenty-six, were native Mongolians and Chinese who served as scouts, interpreters, and camp workers. At times Kan Chuen Pao, a Chinese man nicknamed Buckshot, and Mr. Wang, a Chinese auto driver, helped search for fossils.

The remaining expedition members, twelve Americans and two British, were scientists. Among them, geologists Charles Berkey and Fred Morris would study the Gobi's rock formations. Anthropologist Nels Nelson would document its people's way of life. Topographer L. B. Roberts would draw detailed maps. Photographer James B. Shackelford would record each discovery in still pictures and movie film. Roy was the expedition's leader and chief zoologist. Walter Granger served as second-in-command. A veteran paleontologist, Walt, as everyone called him, was really the expedition's scientific leader. Always calm and good-natured, he had hunted fossils all his adult life. Walt was the discoverer of Bone Cabin Quarry in Wyoming, a treasure trove of dinosaur bones, and was also the first American paleontologist to hunt fossils overseas, in Africa. George Olsen, Walt's assistant, would work at his side.

Being an expert, however, was not enough for Roy. He demanded that team members be "men of character," too. In his view, a man of character was generous, unselfish, kind, and helpful. Roy chose well. In the field, team members might disagree on scientific matters, but they never quarreled personally. They acted, Roy said later, like "a band of brothers."

Note "brothers," not "sisters." Over three thousand

women asked to join the CAE. Its chief turned them down —flat! Roy never took their applications seriously; he may not even have read them.

In 1920, women had only just won the right to vote in the United States after a seventy-five-year struggle. Roy did not mind that, but he drew the line at women in exploration. Like many men at the time, he thought few women, if any, could do scientific work as well as men. Moreover, he believed that women lacked men's strength and endurance; nor could they stand dirt or going without a bath the way men could. "I do not see just where women fit into exploration," he said. "They are marvelous in a crisis, but the petty annoyances of everyday life in an isolated community send them off the deep end." This charge was unfair—more of a reflection of Roy's personal bias than fact. There had been, and would be, many able women explorers. Roy knew some of them himself but refused to give them the credit they deserved. In the 1920s, Mary Akeley, wife of his friend Carl Akeley, played a key role in her husband's groundbreaking expeditions to study gorillas in the Congo. Osa Johnson, the wife of another friend, photographer Martin Johnson, was her husband's partner and equal on all his expeditions. In the very years Roy led the CAE, the Johnsons did pioneering wildlife photography in British East Africa, today's Kenya.

Roy had to decide not only *whom* to take along, but *what*. A scientific expedition, like an army, moves on its belly. That is, it needs the right supplies, and plenty of them. Roy did not believe in hardship if he could avoid it. For that reason, he followed three rules: "Eat well, sleep well, and dress well. Then one can work well!"

A nutrition expert helped choose foods that would keep the men healthy and not spoil. Roy bought a large supply of dried vegetables and fruits, powdered milk, and powdered eggs. Fresh meat would be no problem; there were plenty of antelope on the Gobi. Clothing would be simple: flannel shirts, cotton pants, felt hats, good boots. Camp gear included tools, tents, blankets, sleeping bags, folding tables and chairs. Each scientist would also bring his own specialized equipment. Finally, Roy ordered a supply of guns and bullets. He knew that gangs of bandits prowled the caravan trails of Mongolia. Although he had not met any bandits in 1917 and 1919, he assumed that the CAE might. If the scientists hoped to stay alive, let alone get anything done, they must be ready to defend themselves.

The expedition's gear weighed a total of thirty-six

N
W 22 E
S SECRETS FROM THE ROCKS

A fully loaded camel. Camels carried the bulk of the expeditions' supplies from one campsite to another. Temperamental animals, they might spit at, bite, kick, and roll over anyone they took a dislike to.

thousand pounds, or twelve tons, not counting food and fuel. How to move it around the Gobi?

Roy had seen camel caravans carry heavy loads, about four hundred pounds per animal, but they covered only ten miles a day. Motorcars had little space for baggage, but they could go a hundred miles a day over hard-packed gravel. Thus, each form of transportation offered an advantage and a disadvantage.

Roy decided to combine their advantages. Because camels move slowly, he would send them out weeks ahead of the main party, which would ride in the motorcars. Besides their regular loads, the camels would carry gasoline and spare parts for the vehicles. Far out on the Gobi, say four or five hundred miles, the camel caravan would stop and wait. When the main party caught up later, it would take on more fuel and supplies. While the scientists

did their work, the caravan would move ahead to the next research site. Roy and a Mongolian guide would always scout ahead in a car to select a good spot.

Beijing (then known as Peking in the West) became the expedition's headquarters, because it was the largest city near the Mongolian border and had a railroad that could haul supplies from the coast. From Beijing, the Chinese capital, Roy sent a Chinese aide to rent camels and hire workers in the frontier town of Kalgan. Luckily, he found a Mongolian named Merin to lead the caravan. Merin knew nothing of compasses. He didn't need them. Using only the sun and the stars to find his way, he never got lost. If Merin promised to bring the caravan to a certain place at a certain time, he did—like clockwork.

Roy also rented a palace in Beijing from a Chinese prince. The man needed money fast, and Roy bargained him down to a "reasonable" price. The palace had forty-seven rooms, enough space for living quarters, meeting rooms, laboratories, storage rooms, a darkroom for developing film, and a small movie theater. The palace would be the expedition's headquarters in China. Since Roy did not want to take women along, the wives of expedition members had two choices. Either they stayed in the United States, or they lived at headquarters or hotels in Beijing. Yvette and their two sons, George Borup (born in 1918) and Roy Kevin Andrews (born in 1924), spent a lonely time in the palace while Roy explored the desert.

Twenty servants did the daily chores. Roy paid them a grand total of $175 a month, a large sum at the time in China. They were glad to have the work. The 1920s were a very troubled time for their country. A three-cornered civil war had broken out. That war involved the central government, rebel generals called "warlords," and people inspired by the recent Communist revolution in Russia. Each side fought the others to control the country. Prisoners faced almost certain death.

Roy learned about the struggle firsthand. Beheading, the traditional form of execution in China, was meant to be quick and painless. Perhaps it was; there was plenty of it. While driving around Beijing, Roy saw human heads dangling from telephone poles. Once a crowd surged into a main street, blocking his way. As he jammed on the brakes, police officers dragged four men in front of the car. Forcing them to kneel in turn, an officer cut off their heads with his sword. For three days the bodies lay where they fell, amid pools of blood, as a warning to others. Sights like this sickened Roy. He could not wait to leave Beijing for the desert.

Roy and Merin, leader of the camel caravan, scan the Gobi Desert during a trip to select the next campsite.

Explorations in the Gobi Desert

On April 17, 1922, the first Central Asiatic Expedition drove through a narrow gateway in the Great Wall of China, built by the ancient emperors to keep out Mongolian invaders. Heading northward across Inner Mongolia, it crossed into Mongolia proper in two light trucks and six touring cars. Specially built for long trips, a touring car had four doors, a folding top, and solid rubber tires that would not go flat. Every vehicle moved under a mountain of baggage. Six weeks earlier, Roy had sent Merin ahead with seventy-eight camels loaded with camp supplies, gasoline, and spare parts for the vehicles.

Roy would lead expeditions into the Gobi five times in all. In 1922, 1923, and 1925, he went into Mongolia; in 1928 and 1930, he visited only Chinese Inner Mongolia. Roy spent the time between expeditions at the palace in Beijing, writing detailed reports, making new plans, and arguing with the Chinese government as the civil war raged. In 1926, he returned to New York to publicize the CAE's work and raise more money.

Although Roy had planned the expedition down to the last detail, it naturally faced unexpected problems. Out on the Gobi, Mother Nature did as she pleased. And it sometimes pleased her to be ornery.

During the first visit, in 1922, clouds of sand flies buzzed around the explorers' heads. Hairy spiders, big as a man's hand, hid in their sleeping bags. Then, and always, snakes terrified the team. The pit viper is the commonest snake in the Gobi and is highly poisonous.

One night a pit-viper invasion roused the camp. Although these reptiles are normally solitary creatures, all those camels and people must have disturbed them, drawing them from their dens under the campsite. "Dear God, my tent is full of snakes," Roy heard geologist Fred Morris cry. "There are hundreds of them!" Pit vipers were everywhere—under blankets, in boots, hats, and jackets. Shouting wildly, men grabbed pickaxes and shovels. Everybody spent the rest of the night hacking at the uninvited guests, killing forty-seven. Fortunately, nobody got bitten.

The experience scared the explorers, but none worse than their leader. Although Roy had collected all kinds of animal specimens, he was never keen on snakes. The thought of a snake slithering into his sleeping bag gave him the creeps. From then on, he made sure to take a weapon when going out after dark. Once he stepped out of his tent onto something round and hard. "I must have jumped three feet straight up, and what I yelled made blue sparks in the air. But it was only a piece of half-inch rope!" No wonder Roy named the place Viper Camp.

Yet, for pure terror, nothing compared to a Gobi sandstorm. In the spring, high winds send one sandstorm after another roaring across the desert and south into China. It is Gobi dust that makes the Yellow River—China's second longest—yellow. Come April, clouds of yellow dust settle over Beijing for weeks at a time, forcing residents to wear cotton masks outdoors.

Roy told how, on that first trip, he awoke one morning to see a yellow cloud rolling over the horizon. Each second it grew larger, driven by howling winds, blotting out the sky. The storm hit the camp with the force of a runaway train. Hundred-mile-an-hour winds toppled tents and sent their contents flying in all directions at once. Wind gusts brought blizzards of sand and gravel. Sand got into the men's hair and their boots. It even got into their underwear, rubbing their skin raw. If a man raised his head to call a companion, his mouth and nose instantly filled with sand.

The wind tore Roy's shirt off his back, lashing his flesh with sand until it bled. *Sleep was impossible,* he wrote later. *Seemingly a raging devil stood beside my head with buckets of sand, ready to dash them into my face the moment I came up for air out of the sleeping bag. After each raging attack, it would draw off for a few moments' rest. Then, with a sudden spring, the storm devil was on us again, clawing, striking, ripping, seeming to roar in fury that any of the tents still stood.* This storm lasted ten days. It was the first of many.

Yet the only real harm any expedition member suffered was self-inflicted. In 1928, an antelope caused Roy, the gun expert, to shoot himself. He had wounded the beautiful creature with his rifle and wanted to end its suffering with a pistol bullet. The holster had a safety catch to keep the pistol from falling out. While releasing it, Roy's finger slipped off the catch and pressed the trigger, sending a bullet into his leg. Luckily, it struck no major blood vessel and broke no bones. Roy recovered without suffering any permanent damage—except, perhaps, to his pride.

To ease their loneliness, expedition members adopted pets during their trips to the Gobi. One fellow had a pair of young golden eagles, magnificent birds of prey. Others kept a fawn, a hedgehog, and an owl. Walt Granger went

Walter Granger and a friend. The chief paleontologist had two red-billed crows as pets, one of which inspects his pipe.

around camp with a red-billed crow perched on his shoulder. Sometimes the bird leaned over to "whisper" in his ear with its beak.

Roy had his own dog, a German shepherd called Wolf, and Connie, a black vulture he raised from a chick. A black vulture is among the world's largest birds; Connie

eventually had a ten-foot wingspan. Wolf liked to sleep in Roy's tent—unless Connie wanted to sleep there, too. The dog's teeth were no match for the vulture's talons and beak.

Because vultures are scavengers—animals that feed on the bodies of dead animals—people believed the birds were dirty. So did Roy, until he learned otherwise. Connie

Time out for a rest. Assistant paleontologist George Olsen relaxes with Roy's black vulture, Connie, and Wolf, his German shepherd.

liked to bathe in desert lakes. She would march into the water, soak herself, then flap her wings until they dried. In camp, she rapped a water bucket with her beak and opened her mouth whenever she wanted a drink. If Roy ignored her, she pulled at his pants' legs until he poured a ladle of water into her open mouth. Connie liked Roy. "She would poke her great head under my coat and rub up and down, nestling it under my arm."

Camels showed their affections differently. Asian camels did not seem to like white people; Roy thought the camels might have found the men's body odor strange. If a team member came too close to a camel, it might spit a wad of sticky goo into his face. Camel spit once drenched Dr. Garber, the expedition surgeon, from head to toe. "It gave him such a bath of partially digested vegetation," Roy recalled, "that he was washing himself for the best part of the day and even then couldn't get rid of the smell." Camels also had a nasty kick. When a person least expected it, a camel might strike out with a front leg. If its victim fell, it might drop to its knees and roll over on him. Its bite could cause blood poisoning.

Few nomads had ever seen a white person, let alone a motor vehicle. When nearing a camp, the iron monsters initially frightened the nomads, particularly if their driv-

ers suddenly raced the motors. The explorers often visited nomads to socialize, ask directions, or hire men to dig out a car that got stuck in sand. Since the cars did them no harm, the people quickly lost their fear.

Nomads would gather around the strangers, who seemed like visitors from another world. Roy gave them a few token gifts as signs of friendship. Women prized mirrors; some saw their images in them for the first time. Men favored cigarettes.

Roy's men liked to entertain them. A scientist who had a complete set of false teeth usually started the "show." He rolled up his sleeves, spread his hands, and pointed to his teeth. Then with a shout he yanked them out and held them over his head. The nomads could hardly believe their eyes; when an adult Mongolian lost a tooth, it stayed lost. Another scientist had a glass eye. After mumbling some nonsense words, he pulled it out, showed it to the crowd, and popped it in again. With that, the nomads asked a logical question: Could white men also take off their arms and legs? Roy said they could but were too tired to continue. Mongolian entertainers performed different sorts of tricks at festivals, so the nomads knew there was nothing "magical" about the Americans' tricks. Everybody laughed.

Nomads put on shows of their own. Roy found these as

Mechanic Norman Lovell works on expedition vehicles while two Mongolian interpreters watch. Heat, dust, and rough terrain made it necessary to inspect and repair vehicles often.

Mongolian women and children standing outside their yurt, a kind of tent made of sheets of felt stretched over a wooden frame. Highly portable, a yurt could be taken down or set up in thirty minutes.

exciting as any rodeos he'd seen back home. Men raced horses, rode bucking broncos, and held roping contests. Unlike American cowboys, they did not use lassos. Instead, they had a long birch pole, thin as a fishing rod, with a rope noose at the end. To catch an animal, they galloped behind it and slipped the loop over its neck. After the show,

the headman usually invited the strangers to a feast.

Like all people living in harsh places where food is scarce, the nomads thought it sinful to waste a morsel. For them, anything that gave nourishment was precious. Besides, they had grown up with a certain diet, and it tasted just fine to them. However, visitors from countries where food is more plentiful might have a different opinion. The scientists never got used to Mongolian food.

Roy, for one, found Mongolian food hard to eat. Once he and auto mechanic MacKenzie Young went to dinner in a yurt, a kind of tent. In the center, they saw a huge iron kettle hanging over a fire of *argul*—bricks of dried dung. (Since there were few trees on the Gobi, nomads used dried animal dung for fuel. In winter, they built dung walls around their yurts to keep out the cold wind.) The kettle held an entire sheep.

Their host offered them what he considered the best part of the sheep, a courtesy due to honored guests. Reaching into the kettle, he fished out the head and handed it to Roy. It was bright red, because his wife had taken off its fur. Roy saw two eyes staring up at him. He knew he was supposed to dig one out with the point of his knife, pop it into his mouth, and say it tasted delicious. Although he felt like vomiting, he had to be polite. Refusing to eat the eye would have offended his host. At last, he got the eye into his mouth and passed the head to his companion. "Go to it, old-timer," Roy murmured out of the corner of his mouth. "Dig into it."

Mac dug in—and nearly choked. Yet he managed to keep the eye in his mouth. Luckily, their host turned away

for a moment. Roy quickly put the eye into his pocket. So did Mac.

The rest of the meal consisted of slabs of boiled sheep washed down with a mixture of strong tea and melted butter. Returning to camp after dinner, the two men stopped near some flat stones. "On our way home, Mac and I solemnly produced the sheep's eyes from our respective pockets and with the greatest satisfaction threw them as hard as we could against a stone slab. They spattered beautifully!" Yet, had their host seen them, he would have been greatly offended by their ingratitude and bad manners.

On the CAE's second visit to the Gobi, in 1923, bandits offered bullets instead of food. Roy ran into these criminals several times. Roy and Mac once drove in separate cars to Kalgan for extra supplies. On the return trip, Roy went a few miles ahead of Mac. Separating from his companion proved a mistake. Before long, Roy saw a horseman on a hilltop, the sun glinting off the barrel of a rifle. Now, in the Gobi, bandits were usually the only people with rifles. Roy had two six-shooters in holsters on his belt. Instantly, he drew a pistol and fired warning shots. The rider took the hint and galloped away.

As his car topped the rim of a small valley, Roy sucked in his breath. Looking down, his heart began pounding with fear and excitement. There, waiting for him at the base of the slope, were four mounted bandits. "I'm in for it now," he told himself.

Since the trail was too narrow to allow for turning the car around, Roy knew he must fight. He also knew that no Mongolian horse would stand up to a charging car. So he leaned on the horn and stepped on the gas. The car roared downhill amid a cloud of dust. In Roy's words:

The expected happened! While the brigands were endeavoring to unship their rifles, which were on their backs, their horses began a series of leaps and bounds, madly bucking and rearing, so that the men could hardly stay in their saddles. I opened up with one of my six-shooters, firing close to their heads, and in a second the situation had changed! The only thing the brigands wanted to do was to get away. When last I saw them, they were breaking all speed records on the other side of the valley. It would have been easy to kill them all, but I did not wish to shoot them in cold blood, and contented myself with giving them the worst fright of their lives.

The explorer would not shoot another person, not even an armed bandit, unless it was absolutely necessary to save his own life.

Roy found brushes with bandits exciting—*too* exciting to be fun. Yet they were dull compared to fossil hunting.

Dinosaurs of the Flaming Cliffs

Walt Granger had a golden rule for fossil hunters: "Never dig for bones unless you see them." It proved to be a very good rule. Paleontologists follow it to this day.

Sometimes, without searching for fossils, hikers find them in rocks lying on the ground. That is just plain luck.

Yet if you dig just anywhere, you are almost certain not to find fossils. There is no point searching in rocks formed by volcanoes. A volcano's heat melts nearby rocks, destroying any fossils they may hold. Since fossils form in layers of sedimentary rock, it is a good idea to look for them there.

Paleontologists search for fossil-bearing sedimentary

rocks in badlands. Badlands are not bad places—unhealthy or dangerous. They are merely barren areas broken by gullies and ravines, steep-sided valleys formed by swift streams and heavy downpours of rain.

Roy likened badlands to layer cakes with nuts—fossils—baked into them. Like the cakes, when cut crosswise they show a cross section of the rock layers. Wind and water, heat and frost attack any exposed rocks. Eventually, particles of rock break loose. Wind and water carry these particles away to form soil or other layers of sediment. This constant wearing away may take thousands, even millions, of years. Meanwhile, fossils "weather out" and fall to the ground below as the rocks around them crumble.

Paleontologists walk over the ground with their heads down, looking for fossil bones or bits of bone. They may also scan the exposed rock layers above and on either side of a gully with field glasses to locate bones. Digging begins only when they spot a bone peeking out of the rocks.

April 20, 1922, was the expedition's third day on the Gobi. Later, Roy would think of it as a lucky day. That afternoon, he made camp near a dry streambed cut deeply into the surrounding plain. Walt Granger and two assistants left the party to search for fossils.

Toward sundown, the paleontologists' car roared into

Paleontologists do not find fossils just by picking a spot and digging there. Instead, they look for fossils that wind and rain have weathered out of the rocks that hold them. Here Walter Granger inspects a fossil exposed by wind and rain on the wall of a steep-sided gully.

camp and screeched to a stop before Roy's tent. Granger leaped out, his blue eyes shining with excitement. Silently, he dug into his pockets. Out came bits of bone that had turned into rock. Fossils! His assistants did the same. Altogether, they had collected fifty pounds of bone in an hour. "Well, Roy, we've done it," said Granger, grinning from ear to ear. "The stuff is here."

Although the bone fragments were too small to identify, that did not matter. For the expedition had found hints that Dr. Orborn's theory might just be true. Central Asia might be the mother of all animal life on land. Overjoyed, the men laughed, shouted, and shook hands. "We pounded each other on the back and did all the things men do when they are happy," Roy recalled.

The next morning, as Roy finished breakfast, geologist Charles Berkey rushed into camp. He and Walt Granger had gone out earlier to explore a certain gully. Already they had made an important find. Asked what it was, Berkey just said, "Come with me." Roy must see for himself.

Roy found Granger down on his knees, going over something with a camel-hair brush. "Take a look at it and see what you make of it," said the veteran paleontologist. Roy saw part of a big leg bone embedded in the rock. From his study of zoology, he knew that the bone belonged to a reptile, but one of a special kind. A dinosaur!

All dinosaurs were reptiles, but not all reptiles were dinosaurs. Reptiles date back at least 300 million years. About 225 million years ago, a new group of reptiles appeared, the dinosaurs. Although we do not know exactly where they first appeared, or how, eventually they spread worldwide. Like their reptile cousins, dinosaurs had scaly skin, hatched young from eggs, and were probably cold-blooded; that is, their body temperature changed with that of their surroundings, as with modern-day lizards, crocodiles, turtles, and snakes.

Dinosaurs had four limbs, but many walked only on their two hind legs, leaving the forelegs free to grasp prey with claws that grew at the ends of their toes. Although some dinosaurs were huge, weighing over 120 tons, others weighed just a few ounces. *Mussasaurus* ("mouse lizard") would have fit into the palm of your hand, although its fossil may be just that of a baby dinosaur.

Paleontologists today know a great deal about dinosaur body structure, yet much else about them remains a mystery. Because there were no humans around to observe how they lived, no one can say for sure how dinosaurs sounded, how they mated, what color they were, or how males and females differed in appearance. Scientists are not even sure if they were cold-blooded. Some argue that some dinosaurs may have been warm-blooded (like mice and whales—and humans), with body temperatures that are stable independently of the surroundings.

Dinosaurs lived during the Mesozoic ("middle-life") era. Scientists divide our planet's history into large time units called "eras," and eras into smaller units called "periods." Each era marks important changes: movements of continents, the birth of mountain ranges and deserts, the rise and fall of sea levels, changes in Earth's climate. Each era also marks the appearance of new forms of life. Species constantly die out and others take their place. Certain species have vanished after only a short time, while others survived for millions of years. The Mesozoic Era, or Age of Reptiles, lasted from 225 million to 65 million years ago. This was the time when dinosaurs and other giant reptiles, their cousins, dominated the land, sea, and air.

Paleontologists have identified the remains of some eight hundred different species of dinosaurs since the 1870s, when scientific study of them began in earnest. This may sound like a lot of species, but it is just a small part, perhaps less than one-tenth, of the dinosaur species believed to have existed. Of these, the findings of Roy's expeditions added many important species.

Early in September 1922, the CAE came to a badland scooped out of the desert floor by wind and water. In this natural basin, ravines branched off in every direction. Red sandstone cliffs, shaped like castle towers and church spires, reached skyward. In the early morning and late afternoon, the sun's rays made the cliffs look like masses of glowing fire. For that reason Roy named them the Flaming Cliffs.

The Flaming Cliffs are in south-central Mongolia, just east of the Altai Mountains. The area proved to be fossil hunters' heaven. Nearly eighty years after Roy first saw them, they still offer rich prizes. Roy did not know it then, but his team would return to this marvelous place repeatedly.

The tents were pitched . . . and every available man of the expedition, native and foreign, went down into the badlands, he wrote. Success came on the first day—and kept coming. Fossils had weathered out of the cliffs and lay strewn along the ground by themselves or embedded in chunks of rock. Many others peeked out of the ground.

Walt Granger never let the chief work on a valuable specimen. Although a superb leader and organizer, Roy did not have patience for the fine points of fossil collecting. "Usually I am banished from the immediate vicinity

of an important specimen," he admitted. "I can find fossils right enough, but my impetuous nature is not suited to the delicate operation of removing them. I simply cannot work for hours or days, as the others do, before I even know what is there." Instead of taking his time, Roy would bang away with a pickaxe! Although his pickaxe methods brought quick results, they also damaged fossils. To this day, museum workers say a ruined fossil, or a poorly prepared one, has gotten the "R.C.A."

Granger and his assistants always began by digging around the rock that held a fossil to within three or four inches of the specimen. Their goal was not to remove the fossil entirely; that usually took too much time. After they had carefully outlined a fossil using a sharp awl, to get a better view they cleaned its surface with a soft brush. When that was done, they painted on a thin layer of glue to hold any loose fragments in place. They further strengthened the fossils with strips of burlap soaked in plaster. Once the mixture hardened, they cut under the rock with a wedge-shaped chisel, gently flipped it over, and applied glue, burlap, and plaster to the underside.

The fossils retrieved this way then started on a long journey. It began with Mongolian workers packing them into old wooden supply boxes. To keep the precious fos-

A fully loaded camel caravan arrives at the Flaming Cliffs. During Roy's time there—and later—this fantastic place yielded countless precious fossils, including dinosaur eggs.

Packing fossils for the long trip back to New York. Each is encased in a jacket of burlap and plaster to protect against breakage.

sils from banging against each other in transport, they filled the empty spaces with soft material to absorb the shock.

Camel wool was the best packing material. Mongolian camels grow thick coats to protect them from the Gobi's bitter winters. Come spring, as the weather gets warmer, they shed their coats in strips and patches. So, whenever workers had to pack a box, they pulled masses of wool off

the camels. Yet they had to be careful. "A camel, in spite of its size, is a very delicate animal," Roy explained. "If we removed his underclothes too suddenly, he would very likely catch cold and whimper . . . while great tears ran out of his eyes."

The boxes went by camel to the railway siding at Kalgan, and from there to headquarters in Beijing. When the team returned from the desert at the end of a collecting season, it sent the specimens to New York. There, museum preparators—experts at preparing fossils for study—then took off the plaster casts. Gently they removed the bones from the rocks, using steel probes like those dentists use on our teeth. This is delicate work, requiring steady hands and good eyes. Preparators may use strong magnifying glasses and even microscopes to avoid damaging a fossil.

One day in 1923, paleontologist George Olsen rushed into camp, claiming he had found fossilized eggs. Nobody believed him. Teasing him, they said his "eggs" were probably just egg-shaped stones. Olsen was not amused. "Laugh if you want to," he said, "but they are eggs, all right. Come with me."

Sure enough, team members followed him and saw three partly broken "eggs" exposed on a sandstone ledge.

The brown-red eggs were heavy, because their insides were solid sandstone. Each was about nine inches long, with blunt ends, like a potato.

Walt Granger said that the type of sandstone that held them had formed late in the Cretaceous period—that is, the last period of the Mesozoic era. This made them no less than 65 million years old.

What creature had laid them? A bird? Probably not. For no known Mesozoic bird could have laid eggs that big. Could they be dinosaur eggs? Well, nobody then knew whether dinosaurs laid eggs or not.

The team stood quietly, staring at the eggs, until Granger broke the silence. "I'm darned if I can figure it out. . . . We don't know how dinosaurs reproduced. Most reptiles lay eggs, and dinosaurs were reptiles. Probably they did lay eggs. But none have been found anywhere in the world." Granger paused. He hardly dared say the words: "Believe it or not, I think we are looking at the first dinosaur egg ever seen by human eyes." Bits of fossilized eggshell had been found in France in 1869, but nobody thought they could have come from dinosaur eggs.

What a discovery! Here were the first dinosaur eggs ever to be identified. During its visits to the Flaming Cliffs in 1925 and after, the CAE found scores of eggs, some

J. B. Shackelford took one of the most famous photos in the history of paleontology. It shows about a dozen eggs, among the first ever identified as having been laid by dinosaurs.

SECRETS FROM THE ROCKS

neatly arranged in circles in nests. Like bird hatchlings, dinosaur babies probably stayed in the nests, fed by adults, until old enough to leave. Today, the museum has a few eggs from the Flaming Cliffs on display. Visitors may even touch one through a finger hole in the display's plastic cover.

Dinosaur eggs, no less than bird eggs, need thin, porous shells to allow the young animal developing inside to breathe and, at the right time, break out. How had these eggs survived so long in their true shape? Roy thought it must have happened this way:

The "hen" dinosaur scooped out a shallow hole and laid her eggs. Then she spread a thin layer of sand over them. This ended the job so far as she was concerned. She didn't sit on her eggs, like a chicken, to keep them warm. The sun did that. But, of course, the sand had to be loose and porous so air and heat could get to the eggs. The little dinosaurs must breathe through the air holes in the shell like a bird. Probably during a windstorm, many feet of sand were heaped over some of the nests. That cut off warmth and air. The eggs never hatched. As time went on, more and more sand piled up. Finally, it

became so heavy that the shells cracked, and the liquid contents ran out. At the same time, sand sifted into the shells and made a core. That kept the eggs in their original shape. After many thousands of years the sand over the eggs was pressed together into rock.

While the team examined the eggs, George Olsen noticed the tips of two more eggs peeking out of an outcropping of rock nearby. As Olsen started to brush away the loose sand, he uncovered the skeleton of a small dinosaur lying directly over the eggs. This creature was completely new to the scientists. Barely three feet in length, it had a parrotlike beak but no teeth.

A toothless dinosaur! Nobody had imagined that such a creature had ever existed. Since it could not have eaten meat or plants, the men reasoned, it must have sucked out the contents of other dinosaurs' eggs. That would explain the beak—for pecking out an opening. Later, Dr. Osborn named it *Oviraptor*, "egg thief." Roy and his team thought the sandstorm that buried the eggs had also buried the thief as it dug them out of their nest.

Each day, team members made valuable discoveries at the Flaming Cliffs. They found *Iguanodon* ("iguana tooth"),

Roy inspects a nest of dinosaur eggs at the Flaming Cliffs with George Olsen, the paleontologist who found them.

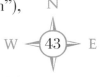

a plant-eater with teeth like a modern-day iguana lizard, and *Velociraptor mongoliensis* ("swift thief from Mongolia"). The size of a large dog, *Velociraptor* was built to run fast and kill quickly. It had powerful hind legs and hooklike claws to grasp and slice its prey. Its seven-inch skull had jaws lined with serrated, razor-sharp teeth. Large eye sockets suggested that very little escaped its gaze. Moviegoers will recognize its type from the terrifying creatures in the 1993 film *Jurassic Park*. Yet those in the movie are far larger than any *Velociraptor* fossils ever found.

The largest number of bones found at the Flaming Cliffs belonged to a dinosaur that grew to the size of a large pig. Weighing about nine hundred pounds, it had short stumpy legs, a thick tail, and a hooked beak, like a parrot's. Built close to the ground, it must have moved slowly, biting through tough plant stems with its beak. It probably also roamed in large groups and nested in colonies to protect its eggs more easily. Since it seemed to have been the most common dinosaur in the area, team members decided it must have laid the eggs they found. Because this dinosaur was new to science, they named it *Protoceratops andrewsi* ("Andrews' first horned face") in their leader's honor.

Despite its name, *Protoceratops* had no horns. Yet the shape of its skull indicated that it was probably the ancestor of a major dinosaur family. Horn-faced dinosaurs (ceratopsians) grew a bone shield, or frill, which reached from the back of the skull to cover the neck. Not only did the frill protect the neck, it anchored the powerful jaw muscles the animal needed for chewing. The most famous family member is *Triceratops* ("three-horned face"), a dinosaur that reached twenty-two feet in length and eight feet in height. As the family's largest member—it was nearly twice the size of a modern-day rhinoceros—this plant-eater resembled a tank with a huge head and a massive bone frill. A long horn pointed forward from each eyebrow; a shorter horn rose from behind its snout. Pity the flesh-eater that met those horns! *Triceratops* is the state dinosaur of South Dakota and Wyoming, where its best fossils have been found.

Expedition members dug out *Protoceratops* fossils of every size, from babies to adults. Sandstorms had buried them all. Today, visitors to the museum can see an exhibition of their skulls ranged along a wall by size to show age and growth. It is the best growth series available for any dinosaur.

The CAE did not find only dinosaurs. In 1925, it uncovered "paper-shales," thin layers of sedimentary rock

Protoceratops andrewsi, *the most common dinosaur fossil found at the Flaming Cliffs. Although Roy did not discover the dinosaur, it was named in his honor, since he led the Central Asiatic Expeditions.*

that separated easily, like the pages of a book. These contained impressions left by leaves and insects. On one "page," Roy saw the imprint of a prehistoric mosquito. After the mosquito died, its body had probably settled to the bottom of a shallow pond, where fine mud covered it.

Although its body eventually rotted away, before that happened it left an exact imprint in the hardening mud. On another page, Roy found "the imprint of a butterfly's wing so beautifully preserved that you can see the delicate veins under the magnifying glass."

The Smallest and the Largest Mammals

Without realizing it, in 1923 Walt Granger made an exciting discovery. He found the skull of "an unidentified reptile" in the same sandstone formation as *Protoceratops*. Although a brilliant paleontologist, Granger was still a human being. Like all humans, he made mistakes. This time he made a whopper.

Museum preparators back in New York City got to the "reptile" skull two years later and were shocked at what they found. When they freed it from the surrounding rock, they saw that it was only an inch and a half in length. They could tell from its pointy snout, used to sniff out food, that it was no reptile skull. Given its size, they thought it must have belonged to a mammal no larger than a rat, probably one with a long tail and furry body. It was a mammal from the Age of Reptiles! Only one other mammal skull from the Age of Reptiles had ever been found, in South Africa.

Mammals differ from reptiles in basic ways. Their name comes from *mamma*, Latin for "breast." Instead of laying eggs, mammal mothers give birth to living young, nursing them with milk from their breasts. Modern warm-blooded mammals produce body heat from food energy, have hair for warmth, and sweat to cool down. Mice and whales, rabbits and grizzly bears are mammals—and so are we. Although dinosaurs were reptiles, their ability to run quickly has a lot in common with mammal behavior. Nowadays, scientists wonder whether at least a few dinosaur species were warm-blooded.

Roy's team was at the Flaming Cliffs when Merin, the caravan chief, brought a telegram from New York City via

Kalgan. In it, Dr. Osborn asked politely, but urgently, for more mammal skulls. "Well," said Granger, "I guess that's an order. I'd better get busy." He and his assistants found seven other skulls in as many days. Not all of them were complete.

Granger's discoveries proved that relatives of mammals alive today were around in the time of the dinosaurs. Most likely, the huge reptiles never noticed them scurrying about at their feet. But even if they had, Granger believed, they would not have paid attention to them. A large meat-eater could not have sunk its teeth into anything so small. Still, could the dinosaurs have magically looked into the future, they would have seen that the lowly mammals had inherited the earth, while nearly all the dinosaurs are extinct.

We say "nearly all," because some dinosaurs have survived to this day. We call them birds. Most scientists believe that birds are really feathered dinosaurs that took to the air to fly. Birds inherited some important features from their dinosaur ancestors. Like the great meat-eating dinosaurs, birds stand upright, have three-toed hind feet, and hollow bones.

The reason most dinosaurs except birds became extinct is an unsolved mystery. Did a large meteor or

This tiny rodentlike skull told an important story. Misidentified at first, it proved that relatives of mammals living today existed during the Age of Reptiles.

comet crash into Earth, changing the planet's environment? Perhaps the lowly mammals proliferated and ate the dinosaurs' eggs? Could a disease have wiped them out? Did most dinosaurs die off gradually or suddenly? Although nobody can answer these questions for sure (yet), one thing is certain. The end of the dinosaurs opened the way for mammals to develop as never before. During the Cenozoic era, which continues to this day, mammals grew in variety and size. Out on the Gobi, Roy and his team learned just how big they could get.

In 1922, Walt Granger and photographer J. B. Shackelford went to inspect a dry streambed near Tsagan Nor (the White Lake), north of the Flaming Cliffs. Before leaving the car, they asked their Chinese driver, Mr. Wang, to wait for them.

Well, Mr. Wang was not the sort of person to sit there and do nothing. He soon got bored and began to search for fossils on his own. And a good thing, too! Almost immediately, he saw the sun's rays glancing off a fossilized bone at the bottom of a gully. Coming closer, he saw that it was as thick as his body and nearly four feet in length.

When Granger returned, he identified it as the upper part of the foreleg of a *Baluchitherium*, or Beast of Baluchistan. This was a hornless rhinoceros that had lived in Baluchistan, an area of western India that is now a part of Pakistan. Indian scientists had found a few pieces of its spine and from them had decided that it was the largest mammal ever to walk the land.

Granger had always felt that the "Beast" had lived in Mongolia, too. Now he had evidence for that. After more searching, he found two huge fossilized ribs and part of a lower jaw. Digging in the sand nearby turned up several teeth, each as big as his fist. Another leg bone measured five feet in length. It was so heavy that two men could hardly lift it.

Back at camp, team members discussed the latest discovery. Walt Granger, normally calm, was on pins and needles. Oh, what the paleontologist would give to find the Beast's skull! Roy described what happened the next day in his diary:

I went to sleep very late that night, with my mind full of Baluchitherium, *and had a vivid dream of finding the creature's skull in a canyon about fifteen miles from the spot where the jaw had been discovered. . . . [Next day] I saw fragments of bone peeping out of the sand in the bottom of a wash. With a yell, I leaped down the steep slope. When Shackelford and Wang came around the corner at a run, I was on my knees scratching like a terrier. Already a huge chunk of bone had been unearthed and a dozen other fragments were visible in the sand. They were so hard we had no fear of cracking them. Laughing in hysterical excitement, we made the sand fly as we*

SECRETS FROM THE ROCKS

Removing fossilized bones requires careful teamwork. Walter Granger (foreground) never allowed Roy (to his left) near a valuable specimen for fear he would "give it the R.C.A."—in other words, ruin it.

took out piece after piece of bone. Suddenly my fingers struck a large block. Shackelford followed it down and found the other end; then he produced a tooth. My dream had come true! We had discovered the skull of a Baluchitherium!

Granger and his assistants took four days to remove the massive skull. It came out in 642 pieces, some tiny as a human fingernail. Back at the museum, preparators needed six months to assemble the bone jigsaw puzzle.

In life, *Baluchitherium* had measured about twenty-four feet long from nose to tail, stood seventeen feet at the shoulders, and weighed perhaps twenty tons. The living animal had an extra-long neck like a giraffe's. And like a giraffe, it probably browsed in the upper branches of trees that grew in the Gobi 35 million years ago. Unlike a giraffe, however, its head was five feet long. Yet size was not enough to protect it. When the Asian climate turned drier, the trees vanished, and so did the Beast of Baluchistan. It probably lived almost entirely in Asia, because few of its remains have been found elsewhere.

Drought also affected the region's lakes. As recently as 15 million years ago, part of the Gobi had lakes, with water plants growing thickly in the shallows.

Platybelodons, or "shovel-toothed" mastodons, another discovery of Roy's team, grazed along the shores. Like modern-day elephants, mastodons had long trunks and tusks. Yet the shovel tooths were in a class by themselves. Adults had two flat teeth set side by side in the lower jaw. Each tooth was ten inches across. Together, they look like a shovel with twin blades. This allowed the mastodons to scoop up plants as they waded in the water.

Roy's team uncovered evidence of age-old tragedies on these ancient lake shores. Shovel-toothed mothers and their babies feasted on the water plants. Sometimes they went out too far. Only a few yards offshore, wells of deep mud lay underwater. If an animal stepped into the mud, it was likely to get stuck. Slowly, its own weight pulled it under, and it drowned. Its flesh rotted away. Over a period of thousands of years, minerals in the water fossilized the bones, and the mud turned to sandstone.

Shovel-toothed mothers might be strong enough to escape, if they acted quickly. Not their babies. In 1930, the expedition found skeletons by the dozens—"a baby death trap"—buried along the shore of a dry lake. Another time, paleontologist Albert Thomson discovered the skeleton of an adult female. Roy noted:

She had died lying on her side and in the pelvic cav-
ity were the skull and jaws of an unborn baby. A
prize if there ever was one! Thomson performed the
[delivery] with Granger in attendance as consulting
physician. The rest of us watched and offered . . .
advice. . . . The unborn baby had a jaw twelve inches
long. In the adult the jaw is nearly six feet in length.

Of course, they were just taking one fossil out of another, not delivering a living animal.

The expedition made yet another important discovery at the Flaming Cliffs. Fierce winds had blasted the tops off ancient sand dunes. Scattered along the ground lay stone tools, the first traces of prehistoric people ever found in Mongolia. Roy called these supposed people "dune dwellers."

Judging from the type of sandstone the tools came from, Roy's team estimated the dune dwellers lived in the Gobi twenty thousand years ago. Even today, nobody has found any of their bones or figured out where they came from or what happened to them.

Yet the tools showed that their makers lived in the Stone Age. This was a time when humans made tools out of stone, mostly flint, because they had yet to learn how to get and use metal. A person would strike a stone with another stone to knock off a thin "flake." This would then be shaped into a simple tool by chipping off smaller pieces and smoothing the rough edges with damp sand. Roy's team found a tool "factory," piles of discarded stone chips buried in the sand dunes.

The dunes yielded thousands of stone scrapers, drills, arrowheads, and hammerheads. They also yielded a humbling surprise. Team members learned that they had not been the first to discover dinosaur eggs. Among the stone tools were perfectly square bits of dinosaur eggshell drilled with neat round holes. Apparently, the dune dwellers had used them as beads in necklaces!

The End of the Expeditions

Roy took pride in his team's discoveries. However, deep down, he was worried. What other treasures lay hidden in the Gobi? Many, no doubt. Yet he had no way of knowing this for sure. He only knew that he might never get a chance to find them. For by 1925, time was running out for the Central Asiatic Expeditions.

The reason was war, not science. China's civil war was growing ever more violent. Communists led by Mao Tse-tung organized strikes in the cities. Police and soldiers shot strikers down in the streets. Meanwhile, the central government under General Chiang Kai-shek battled both Communists and warlords. The spreading war caused the CAE to miss two years of work—1926 and 1927—in the Gobi. Beijing became a stronghold ruled by northern warlords. Fearing mob violence, Roy placed machine guns on the roof of his headquarters. Chinese employees manned the weapons.

In 1926, Chiang Kai-shek sent warplanes over the city from his bases in the south. Most mornings at ten o'clock sharp, a lone plane would drop a few small bombs. It always arrived just as Roy and his men finished breakfast at the Beijing Hotel, a favorite gathering place for foreigners. Roy called these meals "bombing breakfasts." As the plane droned overhead, the men ran to the roof to watch the bombs explode in the distance. When the smoke cleared, they drove to the scene to see the damage and help with the wounded.

Roy nearly died during a surprise raid. He was at a railroad station, checking on a shipment of supplies, when a low-flying plane seemed to come out of nowhere. Instantly, he dove under a parked train, taking cover behind one of its massive wheels. The drone of the plane's motor grew louder, louder, until it seemed directly overhead. Suddenly a bomb exploded fifteen feet from Roy's shelter. Bomb splinters pinged against the wheel like raindrops on a metal roof.

Until that moment, Roy recalled, he had not realized how small he could make himself. "One steel fragment came in at an angle and buried itself [in the ground] within two inches of my face. I dug it out and burned my fingers nicely, for it was red hot." Roy escaped without a scratch. Others did not. A bomb hit a nearby school, killing forty children.

Roy had another close call on a road near Beijing. To

play it safe, he and his three passengers hung a large American flag on the car. In the past, the feuding armies had respected the Stars and Stripes.

The scientists were driving along a "deserted" stretch of the road when a warlord's soldiers stood up in trenches dug along the roadside. Leveling their rifles, they opened fire. Some fellows cut loose with a machine gun.

"Everyone down in the car!" Roy shouted.

That was fine for the passengers. While they crouched on the floor, Roy, the driver, sat erect, a perfect target.

Instantly he slammed on the brakes, made a screeching U-turn, and headed for Beijing at top speed. It felt like riding through a shooting gallery, with himself as the target. Bullets kicked up dust on the road in front and behind the car. Bullets grazed the steering wheel. Worse, Roy saw a soldier aim a rifle directly at him. This one, he thought, will surely get me. "My tummy took a nosedive. I ducked my head just as he fired, and his bullet went through the brim of my hat. That was the closest call any of us had."

By a miracle, nobody got hurt. Thankful for their good luck, they drove to the Beijing Hotel to celebrate with warm baths, fresh clothes, and hot meals. Roy, who did not scare easily, was in no mood to celebrate. *My hands were shaking so that I actually couldn't hold* [a] *glass,* he wrote.

I was trembling all over and felt awfully weak and sick.

Roy led his team to the Gobi of Inner Mongolia in 1928. Meanwhile, Chiang Kai-shek's forces captured Beijing. When the CAE returned to the city in the fall, the government seized its specimens, charging that the Americans had spied for the warlords. That was untrue. However, Roy had sold a dinosaur egg for $5,000 to raise money for the museum, which outraged Chinese officials. In their eyes, the expedition was just a get-rich-quick scheme run by "foreign devils." Instead of gold or oil, it was after fossil treasures.

Roy spent the year 1929 arguing with the Chinese. Finally he wrote to J. P. Morgan in New York for help. Morgan's company was lending millions of dollars to the Beijing government, so Morgan could apply pressure in Roy's favor. Unless the government did the "right thing," the banker said, well. . . . Roy got the fossils back. Although the Chinese resented such pressure, they needed money more than fossils.

Conditions in China worsened, but Roy refused to give up. He stayed in Beijing to organize another trip into the Gobi of Inner Mongolia. His team made valuable discoveries there in 1930, but all the team members knew they had reached the end of their adventure. The CAE faced

too many problems, too many dangers, to go on.

On their last day in the desert, Walt Granger and Roy stood before the tent they had shared, staring at a pile of fossils in plaster jackets. As the sun dipped low in the west, Walt turned to his friend. "Roy," he said, "we've given the Gobi some of the best years of our lives, but the desert has paid its debt." Roy agreed. Next morning, as the drivers revved their engines, a strange feeling came over the explorer. Deep down, Roy knew he would never see the Gobi again.

He also knew that the CAE had failed in its main purpose. Roy's team found no evidence that Central Asia was the birthplace of all human and animal life on land. As Stone Age people, the dune dwellers were certainly human beings like us. Like us, they were problem-solvers, creators of art, and inventors of technology. Today, most scientists believe that the first humanlike creatures appeared about two million years ago in Africa. From there, they spread across the world, evolving into the human beings we know today.

Still, Roy had good reason to be proud. The CAE had written a glorious chapter in the history of science and exploration. It showed that the team approach to exploring worked, and it proved the value of motor vehicles in explo-

The Central Asiatic Expeditions driving through the part of the Gobi Desert that lies in Chinese Inner Mongolia. Sometimes the expeditions had an escort of Chinese soldiers to protect them from outlaws.

ration. Better yet, no American overseas expedition could boast of having made so many major discoveries.

The CAE had discovered the first known dinosaur eggs, new dinosaur species, and some of the oldest known mammals. It found evidence of Stone Age people and mapped the country in which they had lived. As if that were not enough, it sent the museum specimens of a wide range of living creatures from Mongolia and China: ten thousand mammals, eight thousand reptiles, and eight thousand fish. Visitors to the museum library may view fifty thousand feet of movie film and thousands of still pictures taken by expedition photographers, chiefly J. B. Shackelford. They can read Roy's field notes in his own handwriting. These cover hundreds of pages and fill six large boxes in the museum library.

Roy called his CAE years the most productive in his life. That was not because of his own work as a scientist; it was not very important. Apart from the *Baluchitherium* skull, others made the major discoveries. Roy's talent lay in organization and leadership, the ability to form a team and focus it on a goal. He was also a promoter, one who created public excitement about dinosaurs and the museum's work.

The chief got the credit, perhaps unfairly, for the

team's success. Their achievements made Roy Chapman Andrews a celebrity. Universities gave him honorary degrees of doctor of philosophy. Scientific societies gave him medals. The Explorers Club elected him president. Newspaper reporters wrote glowingly of Roy Chapman Andrews, "the dragon hunter." Rich people asked him for personal tours of the museum. He gladly obliged, since a generous contribution usually followed each tour.

Yet success had a bittersweet taste. Roy's total dedication to his work came at a high personal cost. During the years 1922–1930, he put exploration ahead of everything, including family. Although his family lived at his palace headquarters in Beijing, he hardly saw them between expeditions. Always busy, "he was almost indifferent to children and family," son George recalled years later. That hurt Yvette deeply. In 1930, at forty-six, he learned that she was divorcing him.

Roy also found himself growing unhappy about another aspect of his life. A hunter since childhood, Mongolia taught him something about himself. Roy came to see the animals he shot not merely as "specimens" for study and exhibit, but as marvelous creatures with as much right to live as any person. "I know exactly how well I can shoot," he mused, "and the only satisfaction I get is in making a clean kill so that the beautiful animal does not suffer. . . . I have had too much of it. . . . Now I am not keen to kill anything except dangerous game. Hunt a tiger on foot and he has a chance to strike back on more or less equal terms!"

A grateful museum named Roy its vice director in 1931 and director in 1935. He welcomed the honor, but paperwork made him miserable. "I did not react well to confinement in an office," he later moaned. "For twenty-eight years I had lived in the field, and I was like a wild animal that had been trapped late in life and put into a comfortable cage. . . . I couldn't adjust to the change." Frustrated, he resigned his position late in 1941, retiring at age fifty-seven with the title of Honorary Director.

Roy vowed to keep busy. Over the years, he had written several popular books on exploration and science. These include *On the Trail of Ancient Man* (1926), *Ends of the Earth* (1929), *This Business of Exploring* (1935), and *This Amazing Planet* (1940). All of them sold well, because he wrote in a vivid, fast-paced style full of action and adventure. His official report of the CAE, *The New Conquest of Central Asia* (1932), is still essential for scientists bound for the Gobi and historians of paleontology.

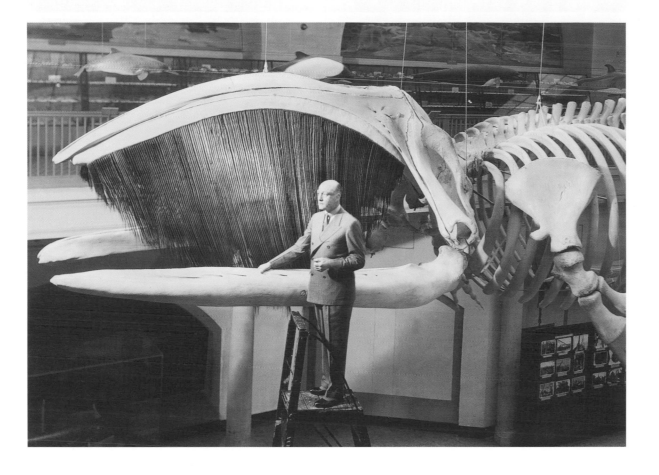

An explorer comes home. Roy Chapman Andrews, in 1934, posing with the skeleton of the North American right whale he had helped recover from a Long Island beach twenty-seven years earlier, in 1907.

In retirement, Roy wrote more books than ever: *Under a Lucky Star* (1943), *Meet Your Ancestors* (1945), and *An Explorer Comes Home* (1947). These were so well received that he branched out, writing a series of "All About" books for young readers: *All About Dinosaurs* (1953), *All About Whales* (1954), *In the Days of the Dinosaurs* (1962), and *All About Strange Beasts of the Past* (1965.)

Roy's books influenced young readers' appreciation of nature. In time, youthful interest in monsters and lost worlds gave way to a mature interest in prehistoric creatures and living animals as part of our planet's heritage. Reading Roy's books even changed some readers' lives, encouraging more than one young person to seek a career in science. Thanks in large part to him, more people are interested in dinosaurs today than ever before.

Roy Chapman Andrews died of a heart attack on March 11, 1960, at the age of seventy-six. He left behind his second wife, Wilhelmina "Billie" Christmas, a young widow he married in 1935. By the time of his death, he had made peace with his sons, mending the wounds of the past.

Following the Trail of Roy Chapman Andrews

Roy once described Mongolia as a vast treasure house of fossils. "It will require," he noted, "a hundred years of work by many expeditions to exhaust these huge deposits." His words still ring true.

Although Roy was gone, his legacy did not die with him. Others took up his work in the Gobi. In reality, all scientific expeditions there follow in the wheel ruts and camel tracks of the Central Asiatic Expeditions.

At first, the Communist nations led the way. During the 1930s, Mongolia allied itself with Russia, its northern neighbor. Russia sent weapons, heavy-duty army trucks, and gasoline tankers. Those vehicles could travel faster and farther than Roy's team ever dreamed of doing. By the 1950s, they were taking Russian, Polish, and Mongolian paleontologists to the Flaming Cliffs. Roy's "pickaxe" methods seem gentle compared to those of the Russians. They used bulldozers to uncover fossils! Nevertheless, each expedition added something important to our knowledge of prehistoric life.

In 1971, a Mongolian-Polish team made a spectacular find at the white cliffs of Tugrugeen Shireh, only thirty miles west of the Flaming Cliffs. Two fossilized skeletons lay intertwined in a block of sandstone. About 80 million years ago, a fierce *Velociraptor* drove the claw of its left foot into the neck of a big *Protoceratops*. In turn, the *Protoceratops* clamped its jaw on the attacker's right arm. Other than their wounds, the skeletons are in perfect condition. Paleontologists believe they died when a sand dune weakened by rain acted like a snow avalanche, burying them instantly. The amazing thing is that fossilization can preserve animals as they appeared at the instant of death.

In the year 2000, the skeletons formed the centerpiece of "Fighting Dinosaurs: New Discoveries from Mongolia," a special exhibition at the American Museum of Natural

History. Officially known as "national treasures," Mongolia lent them to the museum as a symbol of cooperation between paleontologists everywhere. The old finders-keepers rule no longer applies. Mongolia allows fossils found by visiting paleontologists to go to America for study. After a time, exact copies will be made and the originals sent "home."

During the 1970s and 1980s, teams from Eastern Europe and Mongolia also found fossils of several dinosaurs new to science. Their most exciting discoveries were three skeletons of *Tarbosaurus*, the "alarming reptile." *Tarbosaurus* was a close relative of *Tyrannosaurus rex*, the "tyrant lizard king" that once roamed the western parts of North America. Some skeletons are forty-six feet long—longer by six feet than *T. rex*. These meat-eaters had immense jaws lined with razor-edged teeth able to tear out human-size chunks of flesh. The Mongolian Academy of Sciences has the best collection of *Tarbosaurus* skeletons in the world.

In 1990, as European Communism crumbled, Mongolia ended its alliance with Russia. The Academy of Sciences invited the American Museum of Natural History to return. Between 1991 and 1995, five expeditions left New York for the Gobi.

The spirit of Roy Chapman Andrews rode with them. When team members arrived in Beijing, a Chinese student guide pointed to Roy's old palace headquarters, saying "Andrews there!" Two of the team's three leaders, Michael Novacek and Mark Norell, had read *All About Dinosaurs* as youngsters. The author's adventures had inspired them to study paleontology, as it had inspired young Mongolians and Chinese, too. Malcolm C. McKenna, the team's third leader, was an expert geologist and curator of fossil mammals at the museum.

Compared to Roy's team, the new team lived in luxury. Their four-wheel-drive Jeeps could break out of almost any sand trap. Each vehicle had air-conditioning, a blessing during broiling desert summers. While at work, the scientists kept in touch by walkie-talkie. For their comfort they had a gas-powered generator, a refrigerator, and tape decks with a stereo sound system. As they sorted specimens in camp, rock-and-roll music blared over the speakers. Wearing khaki clothes and baseball caps, each scientist kept his field notes on a laptop computer.

Nevertheless, they learned just how dangerous the Gobi could be. In 1991, they felt just as Roy had—terrified—when a sandstorm struck. It caught Michael Novacek and Mark Norell while driving in a Jeep.

Suddenly, the landscape vanished in a cloud of yellow dust. "The storm issued its first volley, pulverizing the glass surface of our windshield to a milky haze," Novacek recalled. "The sand came into the cab of our Jeep like a hideous vapor, through the door jambs . . . up our nostrils, in our eyes. . . . I could feel the slow panic of suffocation." Finally, the storm passed.

More nests of dinosaur eggs were found at the Flaming Cliffs. Roy's men had thought the eggs they found in 1923 belonged to *Protoceratops*, the most common dinosaur in the area. The 1991 eggs showed otherwise. They are a perfect example of how scientific ideas change with the discovery of new material.

The 1991 eggs were exactly like those of *Protoceratops*—on the outside. Opening them, however, revealed the first complete fossil embryos, or dinosaurs as they grew before their birth. The unborn babies were all miniatures of *Oviraptor!* Thus, it seems, the toothless dinosaur that George Olsen found on top of a nest in 1923 was an *Oviraptor* mother. She was probably protecting her own eggs, not trying to eat those of the dinosaurs we still call "Andrews' first horned face," when a sandstorm buried her on top of them. This shows what all good researchers know—that even "experts" make mistakes and must reverse themselves (if they are honest).

The *Oviraptor* discovery is important for another reason. It tells us that scientific knowledge never stands still. It is dynamic, always changing and growing as new "facts" come to light or scientists view old "facts" differently. Although scientists may be certain about something today, tomorrow's discovery may prove them wrong or make them rethink their assumptions and their conclusions. What one generation of scientists accepts as true, a later one may question or reject entirely.

A story about part of a fossil found in 1969 beautifully illustrates this. It lay on a shelf in Moscow, Russia, for thirty years, ignored and forgotten. Finally, scientists realized it came from a reptile that lived alongside the earliest dinosaurs, about 220 million years ago.

The fossil shows impressions of feathers. Until recently, most scientists agreed that birds developed from dinosaurs, because dinosaurs and birds share physical features such as a wishbone and angled shoulder blades, or scapulae. But the Moscow fossil seems to show that reptiles flew long before the first known bird, *Archaeopteryx* ("ancient wing"), which lived about 145 million years ago. Perhaps dinosaurs and birds had a common ancestor? Nobody can say for sure—yet.

SECRETS FROM THE ROCKS

Each year brings fresh discoveries and further insights into the lost world of prehistoric animals. These creatures still have the power to amaze, puzzle—and scare us. There are many reasons for studying them. Because their fossils are so old, they help us understand life in past ages and how it has changed over time. Equally important, they help us understand our own place in nature and how our world got to be the way it is. Thus, there is always room for young minds to come into a scientific field and contribute new ideas to it.

Life, in all its fantastic forms, does not last forever. Change is nature's law. Yet life is fragile in the face of change. That a given life-form may dominate the planet today does not mean it will do so forever. After all, the dinosaurs ruled for 160 million years—about eighty times longer than scientists believe humans have been around.

Yet we are special. Of all the species that have ever lived, only we have the power to destroy ourselves and the planet that sustains us. Roy Chapman Andrews understood this. In *Meet Your Ancestors*, he wrote: *Like a meteor flashing across the sky* [humankind] *has risen to control the inanimate world, but . . . may burn out as rapidly as the same shooting star, leaving behind only the dead records of* [its] *once glorious past.*

And of itself, leaving behind nothing but old bones, secrets from the rocks.

Prehistoric Animals Mentioned in This Book

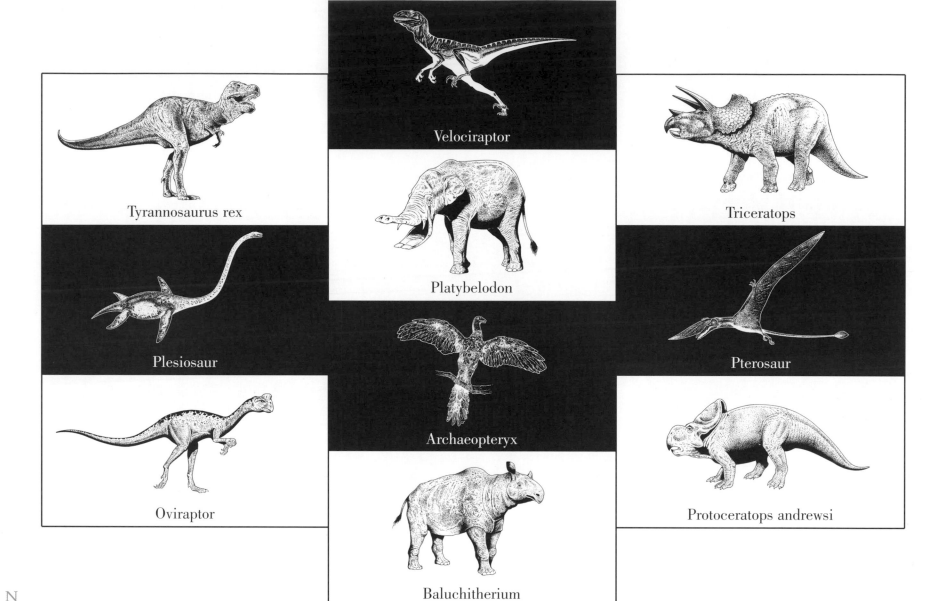

Velociraptor

Tyrannosaurus rex

Platybelodon

Triceratops

Plesiosaur

Archaeopteryx

Pterosaur

Oviraptor

Baluchitherium

Protoceratops andrewsi

Some Other Books to Read

I have based my book largely on the writings of Roy Chapman Andrews. This is because he led the CAE and wrote more than anyone else about it. Other expedition members wrote hardly anything about their personal experiences—at least for the public. Anyhow, I found the following books very useful.

Andrews, Roy Chapman. *Ends of the Earth*. New York: G. P. Putnam's Sons, 1929.

———. "Explorations in the Gobi Desert." *National Geographic Magazine*, June 1933, 653–716.

———. *Meet Your Ancestors*. New York: Viking Press, 1945.

———. *The New Conquest of Central Asia*. New York: The American Museum of Natural History, 1932.

———. *On the Trail of Ancient Man*. New York: G. P. Putnam's Sons, 1926.

———. *This Business of Exploring*. New York: G. P. Putnam's Sons, 1935.

———. *Under a Lucky Star: A Lifetime of Adventure*. New York: Viking, 1943.

Chiappe, Luis M., and Lowell Dingus. *The Tiniest Giants: Discovering Dinosaur Eggs*. New York: Bantam Doubleday Dell Books for Young Readers, 1999.

Colbert, Edwin H. *The Great Dinosaur Hunters and Their Discoveries*. New York: Dover, 1968.

Currie, Philip J., and Eva B. Koppelhus. *101 Questions About Dinosaurs*. Mineola, NY: Dover, 1996.

Hellman, Geoffrey. *Bankers, Bones, and Beetles: The First Century of the American Museum of Natural History*. Garden City, NY: The Natural History Press, 1968.

Horner, John R. *Digging Dinosaurs: The Search That Unraveled the Mystery of Baby Dinosaurs*. New York: HarperCollins, 1990.

Lessem, Don. *Kings of Creation: How a New Breed of Scientists Is Revolutionizing Our Understanding of Dinosaurs*. New York: Simon & Schuster, 1992.

Norell, Mark A., and Lowell Dingus. *A Nest of Dinosaur Eggs: The Story of Oviraptor*. New York: Doubleday Books for Young Readers, 1999.

Norman, David. *The Illustrated Encyclopedia of Dinosaurs*. New York: Crescent Books, 1985.

Novacek, Michael J. *Dinosaurs of the Flaming Cliffs*. New York: Doubleday, 1996.

Preston, Douglas J. *Dinosaurs in the Attic: An Excursion into the American Museum of Natural History*. New York: St. Martin's Press, 1986.

Some Good Sites on the World Wide Web

www.amnh.org

American Museum of Natural History

www.dinosaur-museum.org

Dinosaur World has dioramas and sculptures of all aspects of dinosaurs.

www.geology.about.com

Dinosaurs has links to many Internet sites on dinosaurs.

www.zoomschool.com

Enchanted Learning has tons of information on dinosaurs and dinosaur hunters.

http://falcon.jmu.edu/~ramseyil/paleontologists.htm)

Internet School Library Media Center Paleontologists Page is rich in information for teachers, librarians, parents, and young readers. Highly recommended.

Index

Page numbers in *italics* refer to illustrations.

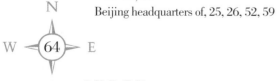

AAZ-5331

FREE PUBLIC LIBRARY, UNION, NEW JERSEY
3 9549 00 77 8085

TOWNSHIP OF UNION
TOWNSHIP OF UNION
FREE PUBLIC LIBRARY